HOW TO PUNCTUATE A SILENCE

Claudia Court

How to Punctuate a Silence

© Claudia Court

First Edition 2020
ISBN: 978-1-907435-91-1

Claudia Court has asserted her authorship and given her permission to Dempsey & Windle for these poems to be published here.

Cover photograph © Claudia Court

Published by Dempsey & Windle
15 Rosetrees
Guildford
Surrey
GU1 2HS
UK
01483 571164
dempseyandwindle.com

British Library Cataloguing-in-Publication Data

A catalogue record for this book is available from the British Library.

In memory of Ma, who gave me my love of poetry

and for Stephen, who embraces it

Acknowledgements

Grateful thanks are due to the editors of the following publications, in which some of these poems have appeared:

London Grip, Orbis, South Bank Poetry, About Time (2019 winners' anthology *Arts Richmond*), *Alternative Truths* (2019 winners' anthology *Dempsey and Windle*), The *Barnet Poetry Anthology* (2019 winners' anthology *Barnet Borough Arts Council*), *Crossing the Line* (2019 winners' anthology *Poetry Space*).

CONTENTS

Beyond Words

words shape my silent self, they mould me
      words recognise my hurt, they soothe me
           gather in my pen and write me

words reach out from pages, they grab me
      words scatter on the wind, they leave me
           return in torrents and drown me

words give voice to wildness, they tame me
      words spill from other lips, they touch me
           derive from lost words and link me

words mean what words can't say, they scare me
      words linger in my wake, they bind me
           redefine themselves and shock me

words take my breath away, words fail me.

The Kiss

The slow stars
are winking
with such leisure
tonight,
sauntering
across the darkness
towards dawn's
first flush.
We saunter too.
There's no rush.

Treading Lightly

Remember how you said you couldn't dance
and then you spun across the floor
in time to music only you could hear?

You said you couldn't bear to partner life
you'd trodden on its toes enough
and yet some silent chord restored your hope.

You said you couldn't dance and then, you did.

Miscarriage

We who would be three
are only two once more, far
fewer than before.

Catching Your Drift
for Micha

I tried them on, startled by the onslaught
of waves crashing inside my head.
I'd no idea what it was like for you, who've
never truly heard my voice, nor even your own.

I tried them in your kitchen, where fridge
and dog and oven whooshed and woofed
and whirred while you stared, fascinated
at my bewildered face.

I tried them because you asked – you wanted me
to know how loud is your silence, and I wanted
to know how muffled is my fondness
by the time it reaches you.

Sometimes, especially at a blackbird's song
or the quiet patter of autumn rain, it hurts
to know you miss it all. But now I think I see:
the last thing you need is more noise.

How to Punctuate a Silence

The awkward silence, eyes
avoiding eyes, thoughts
shuffled, words dealt –

use question marks for what's not being said, asterisks
for what can't be said, or shouldn't have been said at all.

The sacred silence of prayer
lips moving, glance lowered
demeanour beyond reach –

this can be an uncomfortable silence for others so give
it some room, a paragraph to itself, plenty of full stops.

The companionable silence
when two auras embrace
one with another –

such fusion of unspoken thought needs well-placed
apostrophes, to affirm joint ownership of the moment.

The deep silence of sleep
each breath but a whimper
each twitch a spent dream –

if it's forty winks, a comma will do, otherwise allow
a sprinkle of ellipses to mark the pause in proceedings.

The indecisive silence
heavy with ponderance
fraught with choice –

capitalise the dilemma. Split your options into columns.
Add a colon-plus-left-hand-bracket, to convey empathy.

The cold silence of fury,
loaded eyes taking aim
like the barrels of a gun –

create some space: a bold dash, an exclamation mark,
whatever you can. Be careful, avoid the bullet point.

The unfolding silence
that follows a disaster,
air thick with horror –

echo this silence with quiet. Allow each phrase its own
time. Scatter empty speech marks. Italicise the dread.

The floating silence of grief
awash, aghast, adrift
on emptiness –

wrap it gently in parentheses and cradle it for as long
as it takes, each whispered word in lower case, in case.

Haiku

A pair of raindrops
slither down the frosty pane.
Two gamblers shake hands.

Tea at Four

Fuck off, you growl. I've just nudged you awake
with my foot to offer you cake, which you
declined, firmly.

It's four o'clock on a freezing February morning
beside the Thames – you're huddled in two hats
three coats and a greasy sleeping bag

perched on a ledge at the start of a bridge
where blizzards breath unseen through the iron
latticework, turn your lips blue.

Fairy cakes aren't ideal I know, but that's
what we have – supermarket leftovers, genteel
on their doilies. *Can you hear me?*

You've stopped cursing, stopped moving.
I nudge you again, squat at your shoulders
with tea from our van.

I feel embarrassed about the tray of smoked
salmon sandwiches. But I'd hate for you to die
of embarrassment, especially mine.

You grab four sandwiches, ram them far
inside your mouth, all at once. You belch,
drink the tea, your lips no longer blue.

Thinking Without Trace

The lisping child has early seen
that life is seldom fair.
But when I reach your age, he cries
your age will not be there.

The lisping child makes brave attempts
to keep his world a womb –
force feed him with a sibilant,
he'll spit it on your tomb.

Every Last Bubble
i.m. Helen Dunmore

'Pain is yards away
held off like bad weather'

You are worlds away
lost and gone as the tree
outside the window you saw
or thought you saw

as you hallucinated
in the sleep-deprived dim
of your hospital ward,
paper-thin as the tree

almost dissolved yourself
but fizzing on with drugs
and oxygen till every
last bubble had burst,

every last line landed
perfect on the page
and the bad weather
would hold off no more.

One Word

His hands fidget
with a stethoscope
as he discharges words
reluctantly
into the silence.

As soon as he says it
I knew he would.
There's relief at first
to hear the worst, know
that battle can commence.

But that night I crouch
by my sleeping child
wondering how long
till I'm forgotten –
a faded face in a frame.

It's the word I didn't want.
I decide to hear
a different word instead –
his word against mine.
My word is hope.

Moments Before

A tilt of the head, a lightness of tread
a softness of speech, words beyond reach
the cry of a child, a garden grown wild
the playground at dusk, a half-eaten rusk
how memories float, your blue winter coat.

The sound of the sea, a need to be free
fresh sheets on a bed, a plane overhead
the kindness of friends, a path as it bends
the blackness of night, the waiting for light
a hand-written note, your blue winter coat.

The brush of a hand, still roughened by sand
the catch in a voice, impossible choice
a closing duet, the salt taste of sweat
the longing to stay, the going away
a lump in my throat, your blue winter coat.

On Trust

I take the wind on trust
knowing it to be there
by the slant of the rain

but when the rain hangs
in a silent mist, where
is the wind then?

Lifting the Veil

Should I stay and wait for dusk to cover us
in quiet shadow, hide our awkwardness,
wrap darkness round our unbending?

Should I stay and wait for night to steal
our warmth, chill the blood, corpuscle
by corpuscle, drain away the colour?

Should I stay and wait for dawn to creep
across our silence, light the gradual gap
between us, shine truth on our lies?

Love

Whether you're in love
about to be in love
have been in love
are about to have been in love
or have been about to have been in love –
it's always *intense*.

Stammer

Syllables are sewn beneath my tongue,
vowels tighten with each breath. Panic
curls in my throat and I choke on the text
I send to my lips, which shape and reshape
themselves in readiness   in readiness   in readiness.

The clarity in my mind won't translate
and plosives jostle, angry as they wait
for me to break the lock, to find the key.
Others know little of this, hear only splutters
as I hiss, growing redder   and redder   and redder.

Under the Apple Tree

We're on a bench
under the apple tree
whitening blossom
spreading upwards
along its branches
and showering us
soft as confetti
but that's not it
at all.

We hold hands,
not tenderly
but desperate,
eyes forward
tears falling
free as the blossom
neither will stop.

We sit, rigid
under the apple tree
petrified
of the next move.
Petrified.

Being a Potato

I used to be scared of microwaves, thought
I'd be nuked while my potato baked.

I'm better since being a potato myself –
a spud with blight, jacket baked for six weeks.

It's a targeted affair using physics, and tattoos
to mark the spot. Then the daily zap:

Place body in microwave and remain quite still.
All chefs will flee kitchen for safety of scullery.

They promise to serve me with dollops of cream
and plenty of care, but not till I'm done.

I breathe out every last bit of air, then stay like that
till the buzzer's gone – my aim is to flatten my lungs

which have no blight, so they dodge the beam.
I hope it'll work. It's tiring, being a potato.

Night Shift

Evening is just beyond the garden
where fields rise up to the sky.
It waits quietly as afternoon
stretches luxuriously
in no hurry to be gone.

The blushing sun attempts a final
sidelong glance as dusk begins
to spread among the shadows
in that hour of uncertainty
when soil gives off a primal smell
and sounds become invisible.

Dampness cools the air as dew
begins to form on grasses, leaves
and flowers furling into sleep.
The blackbird throats a last refrain
as bats and owls swoop in to claim
the empty darkness overhead.
Evening steps aside for night.

Echoes

I still hear the squeak and trundle of her
walking frame, the crash of kettle on stove
as she tries to make tea with arms too weak.

I still hear the thud as piles of old paper
slide to her floor from countless sites.
She wants to let go but can't, quite.

I still hear the rustling, the swallow
as she prepares to bellow *No news*
in the weekly call to her brother.

I still hear the sigh as another day ends
and she finds herself *not gone*
in spite of the hope that dawn had held.

She's waiting. And it's deafening.

On the Beach with my Father

This one's perfect – a prince among pebbles.
I stroke it, encircle it in my damp salt fist
drop it gently on the shingle
at his unshod feet.

He holds it lightly in his right hand
takes aim slowly, studying the waves
absorbing their rhythm, beginning to sway
with the ocean.

His arm loops back in one fluid arc
from the shoulder, his left arm rising
in counter balance. He shuts one eye
against the sun.

With a sharp flick of the wrist he sends
our prince skimming over the water
bouncing ever faster, until all we can see
is tiny droplets glinting.

He straightens up, brushes his hands together
reaches down to hold mine, triumph on his face
delight on mine. It was a champion's fling
and he is my king.

For Robin

I still remember waking in my cot and you being there
reaching in, brushing my hair   so gently.

Always older, always taller, protective of anyone
smaller – you blazed a trail for both of us.

We did our thing with buckets and spades, itching powder
and squabbles, one or two hormonal wobbles.

I helped you to read books, you taught me to ride bikes.
I told you my fears, you told me yours.

As time passed, you noticed my friends, they noticed
you back. You yelled at our parents: *Cut me some slack!*

Later on, you grew a beard, scraggy and slightly weird,
wore all your clothes at once, just to keep warm.

You'd blazed a new trail in a battered bus on the edge
of stuff, welding and mending, living quite rough.

You disappeared to Berlin, saw the wall come down
made wacky bits of art, held raves, looked the part.

You came back for my wedding – with a troop truck
that spluttered, as white ribbons fluttered on the bonnet.

I still remember the wind that day. You stopped me
in the porch of the church, brushing my hair   so gently.

After that, you blew away.

Think
Musings at a 14th Century confessional

Think who was here
which medieval sinners
and their sins, bowed
low beneath the curlicues
that snake around the screen.

Think what dark disguise
for those who've knelt
or lain, prostrate in shame
at transgressions
obsolete today.

Think who was absolved
by harsher priests
than ours, commending
practices that
mortify the flesh.

Think who carried out
such punishments
yet still returned
in penitence
for pleasures that arose.

Cancel sin with sin.
A·clever ploy to rope
the punters in: while
every sin needs penance
every penance risks a sin.

How is it

you can fling stars into the blackest night
and sparkle with the best of them

or smear pitch across the brightest day
and watch the stain soak up all hope

then fling more stars, while we are left
still searching through the pitch.

You're always one step ahead
two hopes behind. You can't catch you.

When your sun shines, we all breath deeper.
When your clouds gather, we feel their weight.

There's no forecast to warn us of when:
cows don't lie down, nor birds cease to sing.

But, suddenly all that you aren't saying
turns the room dark, takes away the air.

We sit it out, absorbing your sighs
till the storm comes and the rains follow.

When you surrender, exhausted, at peace,
it is then we are swamped by your waves.

On an Edge

Give her a sleeve, a wrist or a hem,
a collar, a cuff, the tongue
of a shoe – she'd give it a trim.

She started off when we were small
snipping the feet
from baby clothes to make them last.

Soon she couldn't stop, itching
to make her mark
a pair of scissors upstairs and down.

Our clothes were measured, tried on
pulled off, chopped up, undone,
all in pursuit of a better fit.

We drew the line as soon as we could
but she carried on
shaping, reshaping her clothes, her hair.

Our last photo shows her wearing red –
a sleeveless fleece
whose sleeves I found the following year.

I saw them when the ambulance had left
with her fraying edges
so decisively cut short.

Getting By

A child plays on the floor
pushing his car faster
as he crosses the hallway,
vroom-vrooming
just as loud as them.

You bitch scream the tyres.
Get off screech the brakes.
Whoosh come the sobs.
A wheel's fallen off
keep going, don't look.

Double Word Score

You were standing at the sink,
back turned, when I saw
your eye – puffy, blue-black
spreading down your cheek.
What's that?

It's nothing, your Dad and I
played Scrabble, he threw me
the dictionary, and missed.

What, the tiny dictionary?
The miniature one that fits
in the bag with the letter tiles?

Lines

I must not play with cabbage
on my plate
I must not leave my hamster
to its fate
I must not cry when teachers
get irate
I must not talk to truants
at the gate
I must not press my mother
for her weight
I must not say her lunches
were a date
I must not say she came back
in a state
I must not count the chocolates
that she ate
I must not mention Dad who
comes home late
I must not ask where parents
learn to hate

Brief Lives

I

She waits, weary, in the aisle
by bread and half-price cakes,
defeated by school, beaten

by books. The tale of how
she's forgotten her specs –
Read me that sign on the shelf –
fools no one, though no fool
herself.

II

You were just telling us
how the school where you teach
has installed knife arches.

Next thing, you're saying
they don't always work
and he's in intensive care –
only fourteen and done for
a dare.

Goreme

Two girls, balancing jugs of water
on sleek heads, stoop to enter
the doorway of a sandstone cave.
Their hair glints blue in the sun,
their shadows throw cool glances
on the ground they leave behind –
hot, dry, stained with the blood
of ancient battles, fought when
Christian swords were drawn
in just such searing heat.

This cave has always been a home,
chiselled roughly from the rock
that's seen so many moons keep watch
along this valley, so many solemn
children labour at its heart.
And always, *Water!* was the cry,
borne aloft in such a way as this
by just such pairs of solemn eyes.
Two girls trailing hems along the sand.
Two girls bringing water down the years.

*Goreme is a Turkish valley of chimney-style rock
formations, scattered with caves inhabited since 1200BC.*

The Night We Drove from Tehran over the Dasht-e-Kavir

The rhythm of our trip
was hit the road at dawn
and find a bed at dusk.
That night, there were no beds.

We crossed the whole desert
and saw no sign of life
nor death, nor anything
but darkness pressing in.

We slithered over dunes
we felt but couldn't see
and shivered at the chill
of desolated night.

Our driver steered this way
and that, no road to hold
his sights, no guiding light.
I sensed the nomads' gaze.

There was no sound but ours
on the Dasht-e-Kavir,
the desert air defiled
by a battered old bus.

Eight hours we kept our watch
for chinks of light, or land
that let our wheels ride firm.
We found our goal at dawn –
the road to Isfahan.

Rescuers

A raised arm calls for silence –
all heads lift up, feet standing
stock still on rubble-wrecked ground.

A child's thin cry below ground
drifts in the dust-thick silence.
Eyes meet eyes, understanding

that survivors still standing
must reach beneath the silence
and face what they find in the ground

standing their ground in silence.

Tidesong

You drifted
on an unexpected tide

carried far
beyond my reach

left me stranded
on an empty beach.

Sometimes I wave
and a wave waves back.

Riddle

I am

the friend whose shoulder
to cry on is always near

my loyalty so fierce
you have nothing to fear

we'll stroll in the sun
with the wind in our hair

and sit out the dusk
in the lamp's soft glare

our two heads bent low
over books we share

until, weary, we yawn
and stretch up the stair

to the land of dreams,
where I'll disappear.

First of Many

Surprisingly small, slightly stained
jagged, weightless, warm from your breath
it sits in the palm of my hand
this tiny speck of your being
freed from the flick of your tongue
and the crunch of covert treats.

I place it with care in my pocket
as if it were a wedding ring
and I the best man.
You grin, gap-toothed, with pride.

Later, as you dream, I will slide
a shiny pound under your pillow.
The first of many.

Disorder

As the damaged wings of an injured bird
so your arms hang limp, frail, unsure,
your silhouette pierced by the blades
of your shoulders, your wrists, your jaw.

How has it come to this? What short circuit
in your thoughts has caused such disorder?
Food consumes you yet cannot be consumed.
You love it, you hate it, it scares you, owns you.

Without it you will die. You understand this
in a way, but dare not do what it takes to live.
As the constant sway of a turning tide
so your courage draws near, drifts far.

In your hospital bed you are held prisoner
while they search for the key to your mind.
They will watch as you eat, watch as you chew
watch as you struggle to swallow the dread.

If I Think

If I think of family
   I think of division

and if I think of division
   I think of species

and if I think of species
   I think of extinction

and if I think of extinction
   I think of loss

and if I think of loss
   I think of longing

and if I think of longing
   I think of love

and if I think of love
   I think of family

Guesswork

You've come to stay.
It's a hot summer's day.
You'd like a shower – sure.
You take a towel, close the door.

Silence. You reappear.
Can't work the damn thing.
Need a hand. Bloody tricky.
Whoosh! Sorted. Back you go.

Downstairs: He doesn't know
how to work a shower anymore!
What else doesn't he know?
What does he know? Who knows?

That's how it starts: all questions,
no answers. Soon, no question.

Up Against It

You stride with purpose
wellies squelching, bantams fleeing
in your wake. Feed the chickens
lock their coop, cock a hoop
outwit the fox, no time to lose
before this twilight ends.

You pour out whiskies
ice cube creaking, soda sighing
in the glass. Drink to friendship
knock it back, cock a hoop
enjoy the buzz, no time to lose
before this twilight ends.

You pause a moment
thoughts collapsing, names colliding
in your head. Think of something
link the loop, cock a hoop
you can't recall, no time at all
until this twilight ends.

Words fly past my window

hover on the breeze
dip, dive, wheel and glide

write themselves on the wing –
there are no birds to describe it

this flock of letters
this murder of verbs, migration

of nouns whose empty nests
still warm, will soon be cold.

The words are heading south
and I am lost for birds.

Lap of Honour

You set off briskly, moving between bushes
beside the swarming circuit at Brands Hatch.

A carrier bag swings on your arm, your father
swings too, your sister keeps pace at your side.

Much planning has gone into this outing, this
oh-so-casual stroll in petrol-scented grounds.

The journey's taken hours, now you scatter
his years, shocked by the weight of the urn,

how fast he streams into the breeze, how much
there still is. All the while, CCTV is watching

as you and your sister dart through undergrowth
tipping, sprinkling, tipping again

your dad swerving full throttle on the wind.
The engines roar, purring his dirge.

~~~~~~

Triolet for Spring
2020

Sunlight through curtains, eyelids, dreams
feeling at peace with the stillness of dawn.
Warmth growing cold, not what it seems
sunlight through curtains, eyelids, dreams.
Memory stirs, consciousness streams –
contagion blossoms, new order is born
sunlight through curtains, eyelids, dreams
stealing a piece of the stillness at dawn.